It's a poem

The Williams Family

BookLeaf Publishing

Presentation by *BookLeaf Publishing*

Web: www.bookleafpub.com

E-mail: info@bookleafpub.com

ISBN: 978-93-95755-39-9

First edition 2022

To all our fans

Hello

Hello and welcome
To our poem collection
Written from the heart

A Joyous Meal

2

Sausage in a casing,
wrapped in warm bread,
Is that ... Cheese?!
Mustard, sauce, and onions!
All my favourite foods, in the shape of a log
Hot diggity dog!

Hello?

Hello! Hi there! Bonjour! Good day!
I'm really not sure what you want me to say?

Howdy! How goes it! Guten tag! Hey!
Gosh I wish you would just go away ..

Greetings! Salutations! Top 'o the morning!
Look here, alright, this is your last warning …

…

Are you there? My friend? Where did you go?
All I want now is to hear you, are you there? …
hello?

Neil

Standing there on the bus
Suddenly they cause a fuss
Secretly they conspired
To announce when you arrived
A call so strong you could feel
A strong and harmonious "Neeiill!"

Big Head

Do you know what I just heard?
Someone whispered a nice word
Now I'm not certain but I think
Their word accompanied a wink
Did you hear what they just said?
Now it's gone straight to my head

I walk around and every day
I hear nice things that people say
And with every word that gets inside
My head it grows a little more wide
Sometimes I wonder if they know
Just one more word, my head might blow

And even then I guarantee,
There'd be still more nice words for me.

Teenie Weenie

Teenie weenie weenie man, why are you so
rude?
Teenie weenie weenie man I do not like your
attitude.
Are you mad because you're small
I'll let you know we don't care at all
Who said mean things for you to act this way
Or did you wake up and decide it one day
You do not need to act like this
Just take a breath and make a wish

iwishifeltsomething

Never finding what I need
Endless searching inside of me
Outside too I have searched
Pointless though it has been.
Exploring, waiting, hoping, praying
That one day soon I find my calling
Strawberry poogle, where are you?

Returning Home

Tail wagging, eyes wide,
She yelps in delight at me.
Together once more.

Sunshine

9

Always there for me
Beaten up and rough outside
But always sunny

Dinosaurs

65 million years ago
They used to roam our earth
Searching for new victims
A way to show their worth
Lurking in the shadows
Waiting for the day
When they could all jump out and say
'I could eat plants every day'

little caravan man

there once was a little man
in a big big caravan
travelling by himself
couldn't reach the top shelf
hands too small
heart too big
poor poor little caravan man

Bertie

This is Bertie
Bertie says "hi"
Drive Bertie
Roll Bertie
Oops Bertie die

Dogs

Big dogs, little dogs
Scruffy dogs, fluffy dogs
We all love dogs
Even when they look like frogs

Drip

Drip drip drip from the kitchen
Drip drip drip from the bathroom
All this never ending dripping
The kitchen sink is quickly filling
No need to turn the tap to run a bath
Just place the plug, watch and laugh
As the tub quickly fills, jump right in and have a
drink
But while you sit and relax, about your bills just
don't think
Yes the cost is a bummer
Maybe next time call the plumber

Cheese

Feta, tasty, cheddar
They just keep getting better
Camembert, mozzarella
They could be nice in paella

Haiku

I can write a....no
I've got it! No, too many.
Ok no, too hard.

Flowers

Beautiful flowers
Blooming again this season
Nice little flowers

Leaving

More people leaving
Once upsetting, now relieving
No longer do I have to worry
About who I'll invite if I marry
No invitations to catch up
Means more time with my pup
But now I fear I'll never know
What it's like to hear hello
From someone new and unexpected
Maybe my social life has been neglected

Even You?!

Even you are leaving me?
I thought forever we would be
But go ahead turn the page
Close the curtain on my stage
If you ever change your mind
Maybe I would be so kind
To stay right here where you left me
Come back soon, please don't forget me

Goodbye

Ok for real now
Thank you for your precious time
Now we say goodbye.